Little Miss Muffet

Written by Chris and Melanie Rice
Illustrated by Katinka Kew

Collins Educational
An Imprint of HarperCollinsPublishers

Characters

Miss Muffet

Spider

Setting

Miss Muffet:

I wonder what's in my lunch box today. Oh look! It's curds and whey. My favourite.

Spider:

Curds and whey! That's my favourite too.

Miss Muffet:

I'm glad there aren't any spiders here. I hate spiders. They're creepy.

Spider:

Mmmm! That looks good.

Miss Muffet:

Who said that? I can't see anyone.

Spider:

If I stretch out one of my legs,
I might be able to reach that
delicious curds and whey.

Miss Muffet:
 Ooh! I can feel something tickling me.

Spider:
 I know. I'll sneak round the other side.

Miss Muffet:
 Yummy. I'm so hungry.

Spider:
    Maybe if I sit down beside her, she won't notice.

Miss Muffet:
   Aagghh!

Spider:
   Hey, don't forget your lunch box!